Anne O. Krueger

A New Approach To Sovereign Debt Restructuring

International Monetary Fund
Washington, D.C.
April 2002

Cover design: Luisa Menjivar-Macdonald
Composition: Alicia Etchebarne-Bourdin

ISBN 1-58906-121-7

Published April, 2002

To order additional copies of this publication, contact:

International Monetary Fund, Publication Services
700 19th Street, N.W., Washington, D.C. 20431, U.S.A.
Tel: (202) 623-7430 Telefax: (202) 623-7201
E-mail: publications@imf.org
Internet: http://www.imf.org

Contents

Preface v

A New Approach to Sovereign Debt Restructuring 1

The Need for a Sovereign Debt Restructuring Mechanism 4

Core Features of a Sovereign Debt Restructuring Mechanism 10

The Role of the IMF 21

The Legal Basis for a Sovereign Debt Restructuring Mechanism 29

Conclusion 39

Preface

Much has been done to strengthen the architecture of the international financial system in the wake of the emerging market financial crises of the late 1990s, both in terms of crisis prevention and crisis management. But the lack of adequate incentives to ensure the timely and orderly restructuring of unsustainable sovereign debts has remained an important weakness. Staff and management of the IMF have been considering in recent months how to fill this gap, helped by suggestions from academics, the private creditor community, nongovernmental organizations, national authorities, and our Executive Board.

I have addressed the need for a new approach to sovereign debt restructuring in a number of speeches and articles in recent months, and the Board has discussed two substantive papers on the subject. This pamphlet is intended to draw together the latest state of our thinking in a single publication. Many colleagues at the Fund have contributed to our thinking on this issue, in particular Mark Allen, Jack Boorman, Robert Chote, Matthew Fisher, Timothy Geithner, Francois Gianviti, Gerd Haeusler, Sean Hagan, Alan MacArthur, and Brad Setser. My thanks to them for their contributions. The pamphlet was edited by Jeremy Clift of the External Relations Department.

Anne O. Krueger
Washington, D.C.

A New Approach to Sovereign Debt Restructuring

Greater integration of capital markets and the shift from syndicated bank loans to traded securities have had a profound impact on the way that emerging market sovereigns finance themselves. Sovereigns increasingly issue debt in a range of legal jurisdictions, using a variety of different instruments, to a diverse and diffuse group of creditors. Creditors often have different time horizons for their investment and will respond differently should the sovereign encounter a shock to its debt servicing capacity. This is a positive development: it expands sources of sovereign financing and diversifies risk.

But the greater diversity of claims and interests has also made it more difficult to secure collective action from creditors when a sovereign's debt service obligations exceed its payments capacity. This has reinforced the tendency for debtors to delay restructuring until the last possible moment, increasing the likelihood that the process will be associated with substantial uncertainty and loss of asset values, to the detriment of debtors and creditors alike.

During the past several years there has been extensive discussion inside and outside the IMF on the need to develop a new approach to sovereign debt restructuring. There is a growing consensus that the present process for restructuring the debts of a sovereign is more prolonged, more unpredictable and more damaging to the country and its creditors than would be desirable. Exploring ways to improve the sovereign debt restructuring process is a key part of the international community's efforts to strengthen the architecture of the global financial system.

The absence of a predictable, orderly, and rapid process for restructuring the debts of sovereigns that are implementing appropriate policies has a number of costs. It can lead a sovereign with unsustainable debts to delay seeking a restructuring, draining its reserves and leaving the debtor and the majority of its creditors worse off. Perhaps most crucially, the absence of a mechanism for majority voting on restructuring terms can complicate the process of working out an equitable debt restructuring that returns the country to sustainability. The risk that some creditors will be able to hold out for full payment may prolong the restructuring process, and even inhibit agreement on a needed restructuring. The absence of a predictable process creates additional uncertainty about recovery value.

This paper seeks to outline the broad features of an improved sovereign debt restructuring process that would address these shortcomings. A sovereign debt restructuring mechanism (SDRM) should aim to help preserve asset values and protect creditors' rights, while paving the way toward an agreement that helps the debtor return to viability and growth. It should strive to create incentives for a debtor with unsustainable debts to approach its creditors promptly—and preferably before it interrupts its payments. But it should also avoid creating incentives for countries with sustainable debts to suspend payments rather than make necessary adjustments to their economic policies. Debt restructuring should not become a measure of first resort. By the same token, however, when there is no feasible set of policy adjustments to resolve the crisis unless accompanied by a restructuring, it is in the interests of neither the debtor nor the majority of its creditors to delay the inevitable.

Of course, difficulty in securing collective action is only one of a number of factors that have made sovereigns extremely reluctant to restructure their debt. Even if mechanisms for debt restructuring are improved, concerns about economic dislocation, political upheaval and long-term loss of access to capital markets will make countries loath to default on their debt service obligations in all but the most extreme circumstances. As a result, it is very unlikely that alleviating the collective action problem somewhat would significantly weaken the credit culture or create moral hazard.

The paper begins by establishing the case for improving the present framework for sovereign debt restructuring and then sets out the core features that any new approach would need to include. It then discusses the relative roles that the International Monetary Fund and private creditors could play in an improved mechanism. Finally, before concluding, it discusses the circumstances when exchange controls may need to be relied upon in the context of the resolution of financial crises.

The Need for a Sovereign Debt Restructuring Mechanism

The Objective

The objective of an SDRM is to facilitate the orderly, predictable, and rapid restructuring of unsustainable sovereign debt, while protecting asset values and creditors' rights. If appropriately designed and implemented, such a mechanism could help to reduce the costs of a restructuring for sovereign debtors and their creditors, and contribute to the efficiency of international capital markets more generally.

Use of the mechanism would be for the debtor country to request; and not for the IMF or creditors to impose. If the debtor and creditors were able to agree a restructuring between themselves, they would of course be free to do so without having to invoke the mechanism. Indeed, the intention is that the existence of a predictable legal mechanism will in itself help debtors and creditors to reach agreement without the need for formal activation.

It is envisaged that a sovereign debt restructuring mechanism would be invoked only in very limited circumstances. Specifically, when the debt burden is clearly unsustainable. In other words, the mechanism would be invoked where there is no feasible set of sustainable macroeconomic policies that would enable the debtor to resolve the immediate crisis and restore medium-term viability unless they were accompanied by a significant reduction in the net present value of the sovereign's debt. In such cases, the country concerned would probably already have been implementing corrective policies, but would have reached the point where financial viability could not be restored without a substantial adjustment in the debt burden. Countries that are judged to have sustainable sovereign debt burdens may on occasion need to approach their creditors for a reprofiling of scheduled obligations. But it is not intended that an SDRM should be used for such cases.

There are two key challenges to the successful design and implementation of an SDRM. The first is to create incentives for debtors with unsustainable debt burdens to address their problems promptly in a manner that preserves asset values and paves the way toward a restoration of sustainability and growth, while avoiding the creation of incentives for the misuse of the mechanism. The second is to design the mechanism so that, once activated, the relative roles assigned to the sovereign debtor and its creditors create incentives for all parties to reach rapid agreement on restructuring terms that are consistent with a return to sustainability and growth. The policies of the IMF regarding the availability of its resources before, during, and after a member seeks a restructuring of its debt currently play a critical role in shaping these incentives. This would remain the case under an SDRM, whatever shape it were to take.

If an SDRM were designed and implemented in a manner that achieved an appropriate balance of incentives, it would provide a number of benefits. Debtors would benefit from addressing their unsustainable debt burdens at an early stage, thereby avoiding the exhaustion of official reserves and unnecessarily severe economic dislocation. They would also benefit from a greater capacity to resolve collective action problems that might otherwise thwart a rapid and orderly restructuring. Most creditors would also gain if the debtor acted before it had dissipated its reserves and would benefit from the resolution of collective action problems that would otherwise impede a sustainable restructuring. Moreover, creditors would benefit from the creation of a predictable restructuring framework that provides assurances that the debtor will avoid actions that reduce the value of creditor claims. Finally, if an SDRM is sufficiently predictable, it will help creditors make better judgments regarding how any restructuring will take place and the recovery value of the debt. This should make sovereign debt more attractive as an asset class, increase the efficiency of international capital markets, and result in a better global allocation of capital.

The Problem

Developments in the composition of international sovereign borrowing over the past decade—notably the shift away from syndicated bank loans toward traded securities as the principal vehicle for the extension of financial credits to sovereigns—have improved the efficiency of international capital markets. In particular, they have broadened the investor base for financing to emerging market sovereigns and have facilitated the diversification of risk. But the increasingly diverse and diffuse creditor community poses coordination and collective action problems in cases in which a sovereign's scheduled debt service exceeds its payments capacity. This leads to considerable uncertainty among all participants as to how the restructuring process will unfold, and contributes to reluctance by the sovereign, its creditors, and the official sector to pursue a restructuring, other than in the most extreme circumstances. This, in turn, increases the likely magnitude of the loss of asset values, which is harmful to the interests of both debtors and creditors.

During the 1980s debt crisis, collective action problems were limited by the relatively small number of large creditors, the relative homogeneity of commercial bank creditors, the contractual provisions of syndicated loans,[1] and, on occasion, moral suasion applied by supervisory authorities. Incentives for collective action were reinforced by banks' interest in maintaining good relations as a means of safeguarding future business. Discussions between the sovereign and its creditors generally took place within a collective framework, with the major creditors negotiating through a steering committee. During the negotiations, the committee performed a number of functions, including the resolution of intercreditor problems, the assessment of the acceptability of the offers made by the sovereign, and the preservation of confidentiality. Moreover, the provision of new financing was facilitated by an agreement between the committee and the debtor that any financing provided after a specified date would be excluded from any future restruc-

[1]Specifically, most syndicated loans contained sharing clauses that provided strong incentives for negotiated settlements rather than resort to litigation.

turing. This provided a basis for banks both to extend medium-term credits and to provide normal trade financing.

The move away from commercial bank lending as a source of external finance for emerging market sovereigns has made the coordination of creditors much more difficult than it was in the 1980s. Many creditors have no ongoing business relationship with the debtor to protect and are not subject to suasion by the official sector. The number and diversity of creditors has increased, with an associated increase in the diversity of interests and appetite for risk. These changes have been accompanied by an increase in the complexity of creditor claims. These developments have made creditor organization more complicated. A sovereign restructuring may require coordination across many bond issues, as well as syndicated loans and trade financing. This organization problem has been exacerbated by the repackaging of creditor claims in ways that separate the interests between the primary lender (the lender of record) and the end-investor (the beneficiaries that hold the economic interest).

Sovereigns with unsustainable debt burdens and a diffuse group of creditors can face substantial difficulties getting creditors collectively to agree to a restructuring agreement that brings the sovereign's debt down to a sustainable level. In particular, it may be difficult to secure high participation by creditors in a debt restructuring that would be in the interest of creditors as a group, as individual creditors may consider that their best interests would be served by trying to free ride in the hope of ultimately receiving payments in line with their original contracts. Both fears of free riding and other issues of intercreditor equity may inhibit creditors from accepting a proposed debt restructuring, prolonging the restructuring process and making it less likely that a deal will achieve the objective of restoring sustainability.

The absence of a mechanism that provides for majority action among a diverse set of creditors is a primary source of difficulties with collective action. Currently, a sovereign that obtained the support of a qualified majority of its creditors for a restructuring that could restore sustainability would lack the ability to bind in a minority that may hope to free ride and continue to receive their contracted payments.

Ideally, a country with an unsustainable debt would be able to reach agreement with its creditors on a needed restructuring prior to suspending payments and defaulting. But, in the current environment, it may be particularly difficult to secure high participation from creditors as a group, as individual creditors may consider that their best interests would be served by trying to free ride in the hope of ultimately receiving payments in line with their original contracts. If more than a small proportion of creditors attempt to free ride, a restructuring would not succeed in bringing debt to a sustainable level, and a default may be unavoidable. These difficulties may be amplified by the prevalence of complex financial instruments, such as credit derivatives, which in some cases may provide investors with incentives to hold out in the hope of forcing a default (thereby triggering a payment under the derivative contract), rather than participating in a restructuring. Difficulties in securing agreement on a needed restructuring prior to a payments suspension also may undermine confidence in the domestic financial system (to the extent that domestic banks have significant holdings of government securities) and may even trigger an unmanageable deposit run.

If a restructuring cannot be achieved prior to a default, collective action problems may still arise as creditors may decide to hold out in hope of a more favorable settlement, possibly through resort to litigation. To date litigation against a sovereign has been relatively limited and there is inadequate evidence to suggest that the prospect of such litigation will invariably undermine the sovereign's ability to reach an agreement with a majority of its creditors. Litigation is not an attractive option for many creditors. It is costly and may give rise to concerns relating to reputation damage. Potential holdouts face significant uncertainty regarding whether the debtor would be willing to make a more attractive offer to nonparticipating creditors. Nevertheless, the evolution of legal strategies has increased the uncertainties of postdefault restructurings. For example, the recent legal action against Peru may make potentially cooperative creditors nervous about participating in a future restructuring agreement. They may be worried that a holdout will be able to extract full payment from a sovereign by, for example, threatening the interruption of payments on the restructured debt.

In addition to difficulties securing collective action, creditors have identified other factors that they consider hamper the prospects for rapid progress toward predictable and orderly restructuring agreements. In particular, concerns about intercreditor equity stemming from debtors' decisions to make payments to certain favored creditors after suspending payments on other creditors may introduce delays. Creditors have also pointed to the reluctance of debtors to participate in a collaborative dialogue to develop restructuring proposals. The design and implementation of more efficient mechanisms for resolving collective action could also catalyze the establishment of a more collaborative framework for debtor-creditor negotiations.

Core Features of a Sovereign Debt Restructuring Mechanism

What features of a legal framework would need to be in place in order to establish adequate incentives for debtors and creditors to agree upon a prompt, orderly, and predictable restructuring of unsustainable debt? As will be seen, although the features of existing domestic legislative models provide important guidance as to how to address collective action problems among creditors in the insolvency context, the applicability of these models is limited by the unique characteristics of a sovereign state.

Existing Rehabilitation Models and Their Limitations

When a financially distressed—but fundamentally viable—company finds that it can no longer service its debt, the company and its diverse creditors cannot generally turn to their domestic authorities for financing as a means of resolving the crisis. Instead, domestic insolvency legislation provides the necessary framework to overcome coordination problems as they work out restructuring terms. A court-administered reorganization chapter of an insolvency law provides the necessary incentives for a debt restructuring agreement (that often involves substantial debt reduction). To the extent that the insolvency system is well-developed, most restructurings take place "in the shadow" of the law, that is, without the need—and expense—of actually commencing formal court-administered proceedings. As is discussed in Box 1 most well-developed corporate rehabilitation laws include the following features:

(i) a stay on creditor enforcement during the restructuring negotiations;

(ii) measures that protect creditor interests during the period of the stay;

(iii) mechanisms that facilitate the provision of new financing during the proceedings; and

(iv) a provision that binds all relevant creditors to an agreement that has been accepted by a qualified majority.

All of these features serve to maximize the value of creditor claims by preserving the going concern value of the firm. As will be discussed below, these features are relevant to a discussion of the design of a sovereign debt restructuring mechanism. It should be noted, however, that the applicability of the corporate model to the sovereign context is limited in a number of important respects.

- First, and perhaps most importantly, corporate reorganization provisions operate within the context of the potential liquidation of the debtor, which could not apply to a sovereign state. In the event that a reorganization plan does not attract adequate support from its creditors and the company continues to be in a state of illiquidity, most laws will provide for the automatic liquidation of the company. Moreover, the potential liquidation of the enterprise also limits the terms of any restructuring proposal. Most modern laws provide that creditors cannot be forced to accept terms under a reorganization plan that would result in their receiving less than what they would have received in a liquidation.
- Second, since one of the purposes of a reorganization law is to enable creditors to maximize the value of their claims through the going concern value of the enterprise, most modern laws allow for the creditors to commence proceedings unilaterally so as to acquire the company through a reorganization plan that includes a debt-for-equity conversion that, in some cases, may extinguish all ownership interests of the incumbent shareholders. Again, such a feature could not be applied to a sovereign state.

Box 1: Corporate Reorganization Model

Although corporate insolvency laws vary among countries, considerable work has been done to identify "best practices" in core areas.[1] The following features of well-developed insolvency laws provide the key incentives for corporate restructuring:

- *First, upon commencement of reorganization proceedings, a stay is imposed on all legal actions by creditors, thereby protecting the debtor from dismemberment.* This stay is designed not only to protect the debtor, but also addresses the intercreditor collective action problem. In the absence of a stay, creditors would probably rush to enforce their claims out of a fear that others would do so.
- *Second, during the proceedings, legal constraints are imposed upon the activities of the debtor and a reorganization plan must normally be prepared within a specified time frame.* As a means of ensuring that the interests of creditors are protected during the proceedings, the debtor is precluded from entering into transactions that would prejudice creditors generally (for example, transferring assets to insiders or making payments to favored creditors). To ensure compliance, the laws of some countries also provide for a court-appointed administrator to oversee the activities of the debtor during this period.

[1]Including by the IMF, World Bank, and United Nations Commission on International Trade Law (UNCITRAL).

- Finally, it is difficult to envisage how the constraints that are applied to the activities of a corporate debtor to safeguard the interests of creditors during the proceedings could be made legally binding on a sovereign and enforced, particularly with respect to the exercise of its sovereign powers, including, for example, its fiscal powers. In the sovereign context, we must therefore rely on having the right incentives in place.

In many respects, Chapter 9 of the United States Bankruptcy Code, which applies to municipalities, is of greater relevance in the sovereign context because it applies to an entity that carries out

- *Third, as a means of encouraging new financing, credit provided to the debtor after commencement of the proceeding must be given seniority over prior claims in any reorganization plan.* Normally, a creditor that provides financing during the proceedings would have the right to be repaid once the reorganization plan is approved.
- *Fourth, a debt restructuring plan approved by the requisite majority of creditors will be binding on all creditors.* The law normally provides for the establishment of a committee of creditors that takes the lead in negotiating the terms of the debt restructuring plan with the debtor. To ensure there is no fraud in the voting process, the court normally oversees the verification of creditors' claims.

A predictable insolvency system enables corporate restructuring to take place out-of-court but "in the shadow" of the formal insolvency system. Such an out-of-court process generally mimics certain features of the formal process. For example, creditors agree to a voluntary standstill in the knowledge that, if they refuse, the debtor can make a standstill mandatory by commencing formal proceedings. Similarly, potential holdout creditors realize that, if they are inflexible, the debtor and majority creditors can use the law to bind them to the terms of the restructuring agreement. In sum, each party negotiates with a clear understanding of the type of leverage it—and the others—would have if the formal system were to be activated.

governmental functions. Although it includes a number of the core features of a corporate reorganization law, it differs from the corporate model in a number of respects. For example, only the municipality (not its creditors) may commence proceedings and propose a reorganization plan. Moreover, the bankruptcy court may not interfere with any of the municipality's political or governmental powers, property or revenue or the municipality's use or enjoyment of any income-producing property. Finally, a Chapter 9 case cannot be converted into a liquidation case. All of these features could be appropriately integrated into a sovereign debt restructuring mechanism.

There are, however, important differences between a municipality and a sovereign state that would have implications on the design of any sovereign debt restructuring mechanisms. Unlike a sovereign state, a municipality is not independent. Chapter 9 legislation acknowledges—and does not impair—the power of the state within which the municipality exists to continue to control the exercise of the powers of the municipality, including expenditures. This lack of independence of municipalities is one of the reasons why many countries have not adopted insolvency legislation to address problems of financial distress confronted by local governments.

The Sovereign Context

Although the applicability of the above models to the sovereign context is necessarily limited, a number of their features—if appropriately adapted—provide useful guidance when contemplating the design of a sovereign debt restructuring mechanism. Bearing in mind the objective of the mechanism—to provide a framework for the orderly, predictable, and rapid restructuring of debt problems in a manner that preserves value for the benefit of both the debtor and its creditors—the core features of the mechanism could include the following:

- ***Majority restructuring*—**The creation of a mechanism that would enable the affirmative vote of a qualified majority of creditors to bind a dissenting minority to the terms of a restructuring agreement would be the most important element of any new restructuring framework. From the perspective of creditors, such a mechanism would provide confidence that any forbearance exercised by the majority when agreeing to a restructuring would not be abused by free riders who could otherwise press for full payment after an agreement was reached. For the majority of creditors, the disruptive behavior of free riders not only raises intercreditor equity issues, but also reduces the ability of the debtor to service the newly restructured debt. From the perspective of the sovereign, the resolution of these collective action issues will make it more likely that it will be able to reach early agreement with creditors on a debt restructuring. Moreover, it eliminates the threat of disruptive litigation by dissenting creditors after the restructuring takes place.

Majority restructuring provisions form the central element of the collective action clauses that are found in some international sovereign bonds. However, these provisions only bind bondholders within the same issue. They have no effect on bondholders of other issuances, which may in any event be governed by different legal jurisdictions. Moreover, they do not apply to other types of indebtedness, such as bank claims and domestic debt. To address the collective action problems that arise from the very diverse private creditor community that currently exists, such a mechanism would need to apply to all forms of private credit to sovereigns. This feature of a sovereign debt restructuring mechanism would be similar to the majority restructuring provisions of domestic insolvency laws, which aggregate the claims of all eligible creditors (irrespective of the nature of the instrument) when determining whether there is adequate support by a majority to make an agreement binding on all creditors. Aggregation, however, would not result in the equalization of all claims for debt restructuring purposes. For example, as in the case of the domestic insolvency law, safeguards would need to be in place to ensure that the seniority of certain claims is protected.

Ideally, the debtor and its creditors would activate the majority restructuring provision described above prior to a default on the original claims. As borne out by experience, avoiding a default would help minimize economic disruption in the debtor country and preserve asset values, including the secondary market value of creditors' claims.

- ***Stay on creditor enforcement***—In the event that an agreement had not been reached prior to a default, a temporary stay on creditor litigation after a suspension of payments but before a restructuring agreement is reached would support the effective operation of the majority restructuring provision. In the context of corporate insolvency, a stay on litigation is intended to enforce collective action by preventing a rush to the courthouse and a "grab race" that could undermine the ability of a company to continue functioning, to the detriment of the debtor and its creditors (the value of whose claims is maximized when the company remains a going concern). The risk of widespread creditor litigation may be less pronounced in the sovereign than in the corporate context, largely on account of the relative scarcity of assets under the jurisdiction of foreign courts that could be seized to satisfy creditors' claims. Nevertheless, there is a risk that litigation could inhibit progress in the negotiations. This risk could increase if, as a result of the introduction of a majority restructuring provision, the only opportunity to use legal enforcement as a source of leverage is before rather than after the reaching of an agreement. This is one of the reasons why collective action clauses in international sovereign bonds also contain provisions that effectively enable a majority of bondholders to block legal action by a minority before an agreement is reached. But, as in the case of majority restructuring provisions, these provisions only apply to bondholders within the same issuance.

- ***Protecting creditor interests***—An SDRM would need to include safeguards that give creditors adequate assurances that their interests were being protected during the period of the stay. These safeguards would have two complementary elements. First, the sovereign debtor would be required not to make payments to nonpriority creditors. This would avoid the dissipation of resources that could be used to service the claims of relevant creditors in general. Second, there would have to be assurances that the debtor would conduct policies in a fashion that preserves asset values. If, throughout the stay, the member was implementing an IMF-supported program or was working closely with the IMF to elaborate policies that could be supported with the use of IMF resources, this would provide many of these assurances. Beyond the fiscal, monetary, and exchange rate policies that lay the basis for the resumption of debt service and a return to sustainability, creditors also have clear interests in other policies, including, for example, the nature and terms of any domestic bank restructuring, the continued operation of the domestic payments system, the country's bankruptcy regime and the nature of any exchange controls it imposes. Depending on the circumstances, the creditors of the sovereign may have a particular interest in the effective implementation of capital controls to prevent capital flight.

- ***Priority financing***—A majority restructuring mechanism could also usefully be buttressed by a mechanism that would facilitate the provision of new money from private creditors during the period of the stay. It is in the collective interests of private creditors and the sovereign debtor that new money be provided in appropriate amounts. Such financing, when used in the context of good policies, can help limit the degree of economic dislocation and thereby help preserve the member's capacity to generate the resources for meeting debt-service obligations. In the sovereign context, new money could help cover the sovereign's need for trade credit and could also finance payments to priority creditors. Under the existing legal framework, however, individual creditors have no incentive to provide new money in such circumstances, as the resulting benefits of a return to debt servicing would be shared among creditors as a group, and there would be no assurance that the new financing would not also get caught up in the restructuring. An SDRM could induce new financing by providing an assurance that any financing in support of the member's program extended after the introduction of the stay would be senior to all preexisting private indebtedness. This assurance could be provided through a decision of a qualified majority of creditors.

As discussed further below, if this mechanism is to be both equitable and transparent for a broad range of creditors, it will have to be supported by independent arrangements for the verification of creditors' claims, the resolution of disputes, and the supervision of voting. For example, such arrangements would protect against fraud that may arise through the creation of debt between related parties.

Among the many issues that will need to be addressed is the coverage of offical creditors. Given the special role that the International Monetary Fund and multilateral development banks play in providing finance during crises, their status as preferred creditors has generally been accepted by the international community. These claims would not be subject to the mechanism. However, this leaves the question of how to treat bilateral official debt; debt that is now routinely restructured in the context of the Paris Club. We will need to explore further whether it would be feasible to include bilateral official debt under an SDRM and, if so, how this would be done in a manner that pays due regard to the special features of these claims.

Another set of issues that needs careful consideration concerns the treatment of domestic debt in the context of an SDRM. Sovereigns typically have a wide range of debts to domestic residents. These may include marketable securities (issued under either domestic or foreign laws), loans from banks, and suppliers' credits. With the growing integration of international capital markets, and the tendency for residents and nonresidents to hold similar instruments, the distinction between domestic and nondomestic debt has become increasingly blurred.

While the treatment of domestic debt will need to be considered on a case-by-case basis, in practice it may be necessary to include domestic debt within the scope of a restructuring that is intended to bring a sovereign's debt to a sustainable level. In particular, the magnitude of debt to nonresidents in relation to the scale of the required reduction in the overall debt burden may necessitate the inclusion of domestic debt. Moreover, nonresident investors may only be willing to agree to provide substantial debt reduction if they consider that adequate intercreditor equity has been achieved—they would be unlikely to be willing to provide such relief if it was seen as enabling other private creditors to exit whole.

Nevertheless, the treatment of domestic debt under a restructuring needs to weigh a number of factors that will have a bearing on the prospects for restoring sustainable growth. (These factors would need to be considered by both the debtor in the design of a restructuring proposal and by foreign creditors in their assessment of the adequacy of intercreditor equity.) First and foremost there is a need to ensure that the domestic banking system should remain solvent after a restructuring, in order that it can continue to serve as an intermediary for domestic savings and foreign financing, for example, trade credit. Second, it would be important to take account of the likely impact of a restructuring for the future operation of domestic capital markets, and, in particular, the possible tradeoff between the magnitude of debt reduction obtained through a restructuring, on the one hand, and the prospect that the sovereign will be able to mobilize savings from domestic capital markets in the aftermath of a restructuring—particularly in the period while access to international capital markets will likely remain closed.

In providing a legal basis for the treatment of domestic debt under an SDRM, a number of approaches could be considered. One would have the statutory framework cover a broad range of debt, including domestic debt. This would make the claims of all resident investors subject to the majority restructuring and other features of the mechanism. This need not preclude flexibility in the treatment of domestic debt under individual restructuring proposals, subject to the ability of the sovereign to attract the necessary degree of support from creditors for the overall package. An alternative approach would exclude domestic debt from the scope of the statutory approach and rely instead on the existing governing legal frameworks to facilitate any restructurings of these claims that may be required. Of course, this approach would not reduce the need to achieve an acceptable degree of intercreditor equity in order to garner the necessary support of nonresident creditors. It would also raise practical issues concerning the definition of domestic debt. Would this be based on the residency of investors, or the characteristics of the instruments, possibly the governing law, currency (or location) of debt service payments?

All of the above features, when taken together, would establish a framework within which an orderly and rapid restructuring could take place. Most importantly, the framework would address collective action problems that have, to date, made the cost of restructuring excessively high for debtors and creditors alike. This could help creditors and debtors reach agreement on equitable restructuring terms more rapidly, and thus facilitate the country's recovery. As noted above, it may facilitate restructurings prior to defaults, thereby protecting asset values for the benefit of debtors and creditors alike. Moreover, if the framework were sufficiently predictable, it would create the incentive for debtors and creditors to reach an agreement without having to rely on its actual use. For example, the voting provisions would encourage early creditor organization, and thus lay the basis for negotiations between the debtor and its creditors. In addition, potential holdouts would realize that, unless they are sufficiently flexible, the debtor and the majority of creditors could use the mechanism to bind them to the terms of an agreement.

More generally, to the extent that the establishment of a sovereign debt restructuring framework serves to create a more structured negotiating framework between creditors and sovereign debtors, it may enhance the value of sovereign debt as an asset class. Over the past several years, a number of dedicated emerging market creditors have complained about the absence of a predictable and equitable process that guides sovereign debt restructuring negotiations. They have argued that this makes it more difficult to attract long-term capital to the emerging market asset class, thereby undermining the stability of the investor base. To provide greater structure to the negotiating process, consideration could be given to designing the mechanism in a manner that gives a creditors' committee an explicit role in the restructuring process, as is the case in most modern insolvency laws. Creditor committees played a major role during the sovereign debt restructuring process in the 1980s and further efforts could be made to facilitate their formation and operation, taking into consideration the profound changes that have taken place in capital markets over the past twenty years.

The Role of the IMF

If appropriately designed and implemented, a sovereign debt restructuring framework would assist in achieving the IMF's purposes in a number of respects. First, if such a framework facilitates an early restructuring of unsustainable debt, balance of payments viability could more easily be attained in a manner that minimizes the resort to measures that are destructive to national or international prosperity. The achievement of this objective would in turn help the IMF safeguard its resources. Finally, to the extent that a predictable framework assists creditors in their assessment and pricing of risk, it will help to avert future crises, thereby enhancing the stability of the international financial system.

In light of the above, what role should the IMF play in the actual operation of the mechanism? The financial support that the IMF provides for an effective economic adjustment program already shapes incentives that surround the sovereign debt restructuring process and would continue to do so under an SDRM. This section addresses the critical question of whether, under an SDRM, the IMF's role could be limited to the exercise of its existing financial powers or whether it would need to exercise additional legal authority.

The Role of IMF Finance

In the present environment, decisions by the IMF regarding the availability of its resources already influence all stages of the sovereign debt restructuring process. Specifically:

- The judgment of the IMF about the scale of the financing it is willing to provide in the absence of a debt restructuring and the design of an economic program supported by the IMF both help determine the timing of a sovereign payment suspension. Before a member decides to seek a comprehensive debt restructuring, it typically approaches the IMF for financing (either in the context of an existing or future arrangement) with the aim of avoiding such a restructuring and the associated economic, social, and political disruption. On being approached, the IMF is required to make a judgment whether the member's debt burden is or is not sustainable. This judgment determines the availability and the appropriate scale of IMF financing. Consequently, decisions about the availability of IMF resources strongly influence a member's decision as to whether to suspend payments in order to conserve its remaining international reserves.

- After a member has suspended payments, it is currently expected to work with the IMF on the development of an appropriate economic policy framework, and to negotiate a debt restructuring with its creditors. Approval of an IMF-supported program often, but not always, precedes final agreement on restructuring terms with creditors. In this context, the IMF currently makes judgments about the good faith of the member in its negotiations with its creditors in determining whether to lend into arrears on payments to private creditors. The IMF-supported program will specify a fiscal and external adjustment path, which will determine, in broad terms, the amount of resources available for debt service by the sovereign during the program period.
- When deciding whether to support a member that is about to conclude a restructuring of its obligations to private creditors, the IMF currently makes two important judgments. First, it assesses the consistency of the restructuring agreement with the adjustment path in the member's economic program. The payments stream that emerges from the private debt restructuring should be consistent with the member's program. Second, it assesses whether the resulting medium-term payments profile is consistent with the requirements for debt sustainability.

Under an SDRM, the nature of the financing decisions that the IMF would need to make before, during, and after a debt restructuring would not change. Consistent with its mandate, the IMF would continue to ensure that its resources were being used to resolve the member's balance of payments problems without resorting to measures that were destructive of national and international prosperity. Moreover, the IMF would continue to need to ensure that there are adequate safeguards for the revolving character of its resources. Both of these imperatives would require it to continue to condition the availability of its resources on the adoption of appropriate policies and, where necessary, on a debt restructuring that laid the basis for a return to sustainability.

Operating the Framework

In light of the central role that IMF financing plays, one could envisage a framework that empowered the IMF to make key decisions regarding its operation. Bearing in mind the key features described in the previous section, these decisions would include the following:

- First, *activation of a stay on creditor action* would require a request by the sovereign debtor and IMF endorsement. Such endorsement would be based on the IMF's determination that the member's debt is unsustainable and that appropriate policies are being—or will soon be—implemented.
- Second, any *extension of the stay* would require a determination by the IMF not only that adequate policies continue to be implemented but also that the member is making progress in its negotiations with its creditors.
- Third, IMF *approval of a restructuring agreement* that had been accepted by the requisite majority of creditors would be a condition for its effectiveness. Such approval would be based on a determination that it provides for a sustainable debt profile.

While the IMF's involvement in the decision making process, as described above, would help ensure that the framework was not abused, a number of concerns have been expressed regarding the above approach. As a creditor and as an institution whose members include debtors and bilateral official creditors, there are concerns that the IMF would not be perceived as being entirely impartial in exercising this authority. More generally, it is unclear whether the international community would be willing to confer additional powers on the IMF.

In light of these concerns, the remainder of this section discusses the benefits of an approach that would limit the role of the IMF in the operation of the mechanism itself. Under this alternative approach, decisions under the SDRM would be left to the debtor and the majority of the creditors. Accordingly, the IMF would have no power to limit the enforcement of creditor rights. Rather, the IMF would rely on its existing financial powers to create the incentives for the relevant parties to use the mechanism appropriately. How such an approach could be implemented is discussed below for each of the main features of the mechanism.

- ***Approval of the restructuring agreement***—It would be possible to rely exclusively on the approval of the requisite majority of the creditors as a means of making the agreement binding on all creditors, that is, IMF endorsement of such an agreement would not be a condition for its effectiveness. Such an approach would make this element of the mechanism consistent with the majority restructuring provisions found in collective action clauses. The key difference would be that, while majority restructuring provisions only apply to bondholders within the same issuance, an affirmative vote by the requisite creditors under the mechanism would bind the entire creditor body.

  This approach carries a risk that the debtor and creditors would conclude an agreement that did not achieve a sustainable debt profile. However, this risk could be addressed, as it is in the present context, if subsequent IMF financial support is conditioned on a judgment that the payments stream in the proposed restructuring was consistent with the adjustment path in the member's economic program and the requirements for medium-term debt sustainability. If it did not meet these conditions, the IMF would be effectively prevented from lending until the member had taken further steps to ensure debt sustainability, possibly involving a further restructuring.

- ***Activation of the stay*—**As an alternative to activating the stay upon the IMF's endorsement of a request, one could envisage a stay that would be activated only upon a request of the member that had been approved by the requisite majority of creditors. Such an approach would mimic, to an extent, certain provisions of collective action clauses found in many international sovereign bonds. These provisions effectively enable a qualified majority of holders of a single bond issuance to restrict a minority of holders of the same bond issuance from enforcing their claims against the sovereign during the negotiations of a debt restructuring agreement.[2] Under this approach, however, the decision would be made a qualified majority of all of the member's creditors, that is, creditor claims would be aggregated across instruments for voting purposes. Reliance on such an approach would serve to highlight the extent to which the problem being addressed by the mechanism is that of collective action.

  A shortcoming of this approach is that, even if the requisite majority of the creditors were amenable to approving a stay that would be binding upon the entire creditor body, it could take considerable time to put one in place. In the context of a single bond issue where provisions exist that enable the majority of creditors to prevent enforcement by a minority, the process of ascertaining the will of the majority is relatively straightforward, although even that takes time. In contrast, a vote by all creditors (all bond issuances, bank debt, trade credit, certain official claims) as envisaged under the mechanism would need to be preceded by a verification of claims process that might take several months to complete.

[2]Upon an event of default, most international sovereign bonds provide that an acceleration (where the full amount owing becomes due and payable) may be blocked by a defined percentage of bondholders. In addition, international sovereign bonds issued under trust deeds (traditionally governed by English law) give the trustee the primary authority to initiate legal action, and the trustee is only permitted to do so if such action is supported by a threshold percentage of bondholders.

There are several different ways in which the above shortcoming could be addressed.

- First, the mechanism could enable the sovereign to activate the stay unilaterally and enjoy the resulting legal protection for a limited 90-day period. At the end of that period, claims would have been verified and creditors would vote as to whether the stay would be extended and, if so, for how long. Although the IMF would not have a legal veto, in most cases a member would likely only activate the mechanism in consultation with the IMF, that is, after the IMF had determined that the debt burden was unsustainable and that further financial assistance would not be forthcoming in the absence of a restructuring. But a key question would be whether the ability of the sovereign to activate the mechanism for a limited period unilaterally might be abused by members whose debt was not judged to be unsustainable.
- Second, IMF approval of the stay could be necessary for it to be effective for the initial 90-day period. Any extension of the stay beyond this limited period would require the consent of the majority of the creditors. This approach would be designed to protect against the possibility of debtors' abuse of a purely unilateral stay prior to a creditors' vote. It would, however, entail IMF involvement in the decision-making process, albeit in a limited manner.
- Third, one could accept that a stay would not be in place until an affirmative vote of the creditors had taken place and focus instead on ways to limit the delay between a member's request and the creditors' vote. For example, as a means of accelerating the verification of claims and voting process, a standing organization could be established whose role would include registering claims against the sovereign and facilitating the organization of creditors in the context of a restructuring.

It should be noted that a brief delay between the member's suspension of payments and the activation of the stay would not leave a sovereign helpless in the event that the suspension gave rise to capital flight. Under certain circumstances, capital controls to stem outflows might be a necessary—but temporary—feature of an IMF-supported program. This is discussed further below.

- ***Maintenance of the stay***—Just as a qualified majority of creditors might be given the authority to activate a stay, the majority of creditors might be given the authority to determine whether to extend the stay beyond the initial 90-day period. By that time, the claims of creditors would have been verified, and creditors would be in a position to vote on the issue. If the member was already in a position to submit a restructuring plan for approval at the expiration of this initial period, the creditors would vote on the proposal, and an affirmative vote by the requisite majority would bind dissenting creditors. If, however, more time were needed for negotiation, creditors would decide (again by a vote of the requisite majority) whether the stay should be extended and, if so, for how long.

The IMF's decisions regarding the availability of its resources would have a major impact on whether an extension would be approved by creditors. Specifically, the requisite majority of creditors would normally only be willing to extend the stay beyond the initial period if they had some assurance that the member was adopting policies that were being supported by the IMF. When making a decision to extend the stay, the majority of creditors would be in a position to judge whether the member was negotiating with them in good faith and their interests were protected.

Would such an approach give creditors too much leverage in the process? The concept of a stay being imposed upon all creditors through a decision by a majority is roughly analogous to the majority enforcement provisions that are found in many international sovereign bonds. Such provisions limit the ability to initiate litigation without the support of a given percentage of the bond issue. But while such provisions bind the bondholders within the same issuance, an affirmative vote by the majority under the proposed statutory framework would bind the entire creditor body.

There may be a risk that creditors would withhold an extension of the stay in the hope that the IMF would provide more financing or call on the member to make additional adjustment efforts. For example, even in circumstances where the member is implementing good policies and negotiating in good faith, creditors may refuse to extend the period of the stay as a means of persuading the member to turn to the IMF for financing that could enhance the terms of any restructuring. The creditors could threaten to lift the stay to force the debtor to agree to more adjustment than contemplated under the IMF-supported program. Such risks could be reduced, however, by the resolute application of the IMF's policy of lending into arrears, under which it signals its willingness to continue to support a program, even if the member has interrupted payments to its creditors.

- ***Priority Financing***—As noted in the previous section, an SDRM could provide incentives for new financing by providing an assurance that any new financing in support of the members program extended after the introduction of the stay would be senior to pre-existing private indebtedness. This could be achieved by giving a qualified majority of private creditors the power to subordinate the claims of all private creditors to claims arising from financing provided after the effectiveness of the stay.

The Legal Basis for a Sovereign Debt Restructuring Mechanism

As discussed above, there would be a number of benefits in designing a mechanism where the decision-making process resembles features of the collective action clauses found in international sovereign bonds. Decisions regarding both the terms of the restructuring and the activation and maintenance of the stay would be made by the requisite majority and would be binding on the dissenting minority. In light of the benefits of this approach, therefore, the question arises as to whether the essential objectives of the mechanism could be achieved through the progressive adoption of contractual provisions that address collective action problems. This section addresses this question and explains why, notwithstanding the benefits of collective action clauses, the most effective basis for the mechanism would be statutory. It also discusses a number of issues relating to the establishment of a statutory framework.

The Benefits and Limits of Contract

The inclusion of collective action clauses in all international sovereign bonds would represent an important improvement in the international financial architecture. As has been discussed in earlier sections of this paper, and has been demonstrated in recent cases, collective action clauses include two provisions that can facilitate an orderly restructuring of sovereign indebtedness: (i) a provision that enables a qualified majority of bondholders to bind all bondholders of the same issuance to the terms of a restructuring agreement and (ii) a provision that enables a qualified majority of bondholders to prevent all bondholders of the same issuance from enforcing their claims against the sovereign.

The insertion of collective action clauses in all future international sovereign bonds would not require wholesale statutory reform. For example, although such provisions are not typically found in international sovereign bonds governed by New York law, they could be introduced without any legislative changes.

Moreover, it should also be noted that, even if a sovereign debt restructuring mechanism was established through legislation, as discussed below, such clauses could still play an important role. For example, since a statutory mechanism would only apply in circumstances where the member's debt is unsustainable, collective action clauses could facilitate restructurings in circumstances where the problems facing the member arise from illiquidity.

However, relying exclusively on contract as the legal basis for a sovereign debt restructuring mechanism would limit the effectiveness of such a mechanism.

First, it would be difficult to establish a purely contract-based framework.

There is, at the outset, the problem of incentives for the adoption of traditional collective action provisions in all new indebtedness. By definition, a contractual approach would require the sovereign and its creditors to agree to the inclusion of these provisions in all future international sovereign bonds, and also in other debt and debt-like instruments that the market developed. Recent experience demonstrates that sovereign debtors facing financial difficulties actually prefer to exclude such provisions as a way of demonstrating their firm intention to avoid a restructuring. Neither have creditors pressed for their inclusion, notwithstanding the fact that they may make an unavoidable restructuring more prompt and orderly. The advantage of giving the framework for sovereign debt restructuring a statutory basis is that the collective action provisions that it would contain would effectively override the restructuring and enforcement terms set forth in the underlying agreements, as is the case with the collective action provisions contained in domestic insolvency laws.

Another barrier to the establishment of such a framework is the transitional problem. Even if all new bonds make use of the needed contractual provisions, a large portion of outstanding bonds with long maturities, including bonds governed by New York law, do not contain such provisions.[3] While this problem could conceivably be addressed by a series of exchanges that retired existing bonds, it is not clear how debtors and creditors would be persuaded to take such action. It is also possible that use could be made of existing provisions that allow for amendment of terms not related to payment to facilitate debt restructurings in the interim. For example, Ecuador recently made use of "exit consents," to overcome the problem of holdout creditors generated by the absence of provisions allowing a majority to amend payment terms in outstanding bonds governed by New York law. Under this technique, bondholders who accepted the exchange voted to amend non-payment terms in ways that made holding "old bonds" less attractive. However, this technique has been somewhat controversial and it may not be immune from legal challenge in the future.

Second, even if a contract-based framework could be established, it would not provide a comprehensive and durable solution to collective action problems.

Collective action clauses traditionally only bind bondholders of the same issue. In contrast, the collective action provisions of a statute would be designed to apply across a broad range of indebtedness (potentially including international and domestic debt, bank loans, trade credit and official claims, if applicable). This is one of the reasons why the collective action provisions of insolvency laws are so effective. To address issues arising from the relative seniority of certain indebtedness, insolvency laws often provide for the classification of debt for both voting and distribution purposes. As discussed earlier, similar safeguards would need to be established under the mechanism.

---

[3]In contrast, if the mechanism relies upon a statutory basis, a transitional problem is less likely to arise. Most countries recognize that the establishment of a new legislative framework that is specifically directed at the suspension of creditor claims, such as insolvency laws, can apply to existing indebtedness. If the approach discussed in the previous section is followed, an SDRM would suspend the enforcement of the original claims by a minority of creditors (either prior to or after an agreement) in circumstances where the debtor and a qualified majority of creditors have agreed to such a suspension.

To address the above limitation, one could conceive of the introduction of contractual provisions that provide for the restructuring of the instrument in question on the basis of an affirmative vote of creditors holding a qualified majority of all private credit. While further study on the feasibility of developing such clauses should be encouraged, such an approach would raise its own set of issues.

- First, such a provision would exacerbate the incentive problem: if it is difficult to convince a sovereign and the purchasers of one bond issue to agree to the inclusion of a collective action clause in that issue, it would be even more difficult to persuade debtors and creditors to include such provisions in *all* forms of debt instruments in a uniform manner. Indeed, a sovereign facing financial difficulties would come under pressure from certain creditors to exclude such provisions as a means of giving such creditors effective seniority. Moreover, it can be expected that certain creditor groups would be particularly reluctant to agree voluntarily to an arrangement whereby, for voting purposes, their claims were aggregated with all other present or future creditors.

- Second, even if all debt instruments contained identical restructuring texts, which would be difficult to achieve, there would be no assurance of uniform interpretation and application unless they were governed by the same law and subject to the same jurisdiction. In the present environment, emerging market countries that have borrowed heavily often have a variety of bond issuances outstanding which are governed by the laws of different jurisdictions.

- Third, it may not be feasible to establish a process by contract that would effectively guarantee the integrity of the voting procedure. Under the statutory framework that governs the domestic insolvency process, a court oversees this process, including the verification of claims, so as to guard against fraud. In the absence of an independent party to verify the true value of claims, a debtor could, for example, inflate its debt stock by establishing matching credit and debt positions with a related party. That entity—which could hold a qualified majority of all debt—could vote to reduce the value of all creditor claims.

- Fourth, it is not clear that such provisions would be consistent with the existing legislation of all members. The fact that traditional collective action clauses are not included in international sovereign bonds in some jurisdictions arises, in part, from the absence of a clear statutory basis that allows for the rights of a minority of creditors to be modified without their consent. This issue would be amplified if contractual provisions attempted to aggregate claims for voting purposes.
- Finally, and more generally, the financial markets have consistently demonstrated the ability to innovate. A statutory regime is therefore likely to provide a more stable background than contractual provisions even if it were feasible to overcome all of the other difficulties referred to above.

Implementing a Statutory Framework

If a statutory approach that creates the legal basis for majority action across all sovereign indebtedness offers the best method of achieving the objectives of a sovereign debt restructuring mechanism, the question arises as to how best to implement a change in the statutory regime.

There are a number of reasons why the statutory approach could be more effectively implemented through the establishment of universal treaty obligations rather than through the enactment of legislation in a limited number of jurisdictions.[4] First, it would prevent circumvention: if the statutory framework is only in place in a limited number of jurisdictions, creditors could ensure that future instruments enable them to enforce their claims in jurisdictions that have not adopted such jurisdictions but whose money judgments are recognized in key jurisdictions under treaties or local law.[5] Second, an international treaty would ensure both uniformity

[4]In many jurisdictions, an international treaty, once effective, automatically supercedes domestic legislation. In other jurisdictions, however, the domestic legislation must be modified to incorporate the terms of the treaty.

[5]Overriding the recognition of such judgments could be achieved by uniform recourse to the "public policy" exception to these general rules.

of text and (if there is an institution given interpretive authority) uniformity of interpretation. Third, it would address a potential "free rider" problem: without a treaty, countries would be reluctant to adopt legislation until they were assured other countries had also done so. (A treaty could be designed that would enter into force at the same time for all signatory countries.) Finally, the establishment of a treaty facilitates the establishment of a single international judicial entity that would have exclusive jurisdiction over all disputes that would arise between the debtor and its domestic and international creditors and among such creditors. Moreover, such an entity would also have responsibility for the administration of a unified voting process, including the verification of all creditor claims. If one relied exclusively on domestic legislation in a variety of jurisdictions, the process for dispute resolution and claims verification would be fragmented one, with different claims being subject to the jurisdiction of different courts, depending, inter alia, on the governing law of the instrument.

What would be the advantages of establishing the treaty framework through an amendment of the IMF's Articles? This would be a means of achieving universality in the absence of unanimity: an amendment of the Articles can be made binding upon the entire membership once it is accepted by three-fifths of the members, having 85 percent of the total voting power. Moreover, given the considerable benefits of IMF membership, it is very unlikely that a member would wish to opt out of IMF membership in order to avoid application of the SDRM. It should be emphasized that, if an amendment of the Articles were merely to provide the legal basis for the "majority action" decisions, as described in the previous section of the paper, it would not give the Executive Board any additional legal authority. Rather, it would give a majority of creditors the legal authority to bind a dissenting minority.

Notwithstanding the above, relying on the IMF's Articles as a means of providing the statutory basis for majority action decisions to be taken by sovereign debtors and their creditors will require the resolution of an important institutional issue. As noted above, a treaty framework will require the establishment of a verification of claims and dispute resolutions process. However, the IMF's existing institutional infrastructure would not accommodate it playing such a role. Specifically, the IMF's Executive Board would not be perceived as impartial in this process since the IMF is a creditor and also represents the interest of the sovereign debtor and other bilateral creditors.

One way of addressing this institutional issue would be to rely on the same amendment of the Articles that would be used to establish the collective action framework, described above, as the basis for establishing a new judicial organ that would carry out these very limited functions. Clearly, a key question is whether there would be adequate safeguards to ensure that such an organ operated—and was perceived as operating—independently from the Executive Board and the Board of Governors.

As a legal matter, the independence of the organ could be established by the text of the amendment itself. The amendment would provide that decisions of the judicial organ would not be subject to review by any of the IMF's other organs and that, more generally, the judges appointed to this organ would not be subject to the interference or influence of the staff and management of the IMF, the Executive Board or any IMF member. The text of the amendment could also specify in some detail the qualifications of the judges to be selected and, to ensure security of tenure, the grounds for their dismissal. One way of ensuring that the judges serving on the organ maintain some distance from the staff and the Executive Board would be to appoint them for a limited but possibly renewable period. Moreover, a procedure could be established whereby the judges appointed by the Managing Director (or the Board) would be derived from a list of candidates that would have been selected by a qualified and independent panel.

It should be emphasized that the role of this judicial organ—wherever it is located—would be a limited one. Specifically, the organ would have no authority to challenge decisions made by the Executive Board regarding, inter alia, the adequacy of a member's policies or the sustainability of the member's debt.

Exchange Controls

In the context of financial crises, exchange controls may need to be relied upon in at least two circumstances. First, in circumstances where a sovereign defaults on its own indebtedness, it is likely that such a default will trigger capital flight, particularly where the restructuring will also embrace claims on the sovereign held by the domestic banking system and the member maintains an open capital account. Second, even where the external debt of the sovereign is not significant, a financial crisis can arise because of the overindebtedness of the banking and corporate sectors which, when coupled with a loss of creditor confidence, leads to a sudden depletion of foreign exchange reserves. In these circumstances, there may be a case for the authorities to impose exchange controls for a temporary period.

The possible resort to exchange controls raises a number of complex issues that would need to be addressed on a case-by-case basis. Inevitably, difficult judgments will need to be made against the background of considerable uncertainty regarding the ways in which events may unfold. Nevertheless, two broad sets of issues would need to be considered: first the timing of the imposition of controls, and second, their coverage across different types of transactions.

As regards timing, there is a question of whether it would be appropriate to impose controls at an early stage of capital flight with a view to stanching the hemorrhage of reserves, thereby preserving the resources available to the economy, including for debt service. This would have the effect of reducing the difference in the ability of investors holding claims of various maturities to exit early, and from this perspective permitting a broader degree of equity in the treatment of various types of investors. It is worth noting, however, that differences in the ability of investors to exit early stemming from the relative maturity of claims is presumably reflected in the market pricing of the instruments concerned and compensates investors for the relative risks. Moreover, a shift toward a presumption that exchange controls would be imposed at an early stage of capital flight could reduce the ability of domestic banks to attract and intermediate domestic savings and foreign capital, as residents would be more likely to hold savings abroad and foreign creditors would raise the cost of short-term capital.

An alternative approach of waiting until resources are exhausted before resort to controls would lean in the direction of respecting the contractual rights of investors holding short-term claims. It would also keep open the possibility that if confidence stabilizes resort to exchange controls could be avoided. It has the drawback, however, that once controls are imposed the resources available to the economy have been depleted, which will have adverse effects on the pace of recovery and capacity to generate resources for debt service.

A second question relates to the scope of the controls. In cases where a member has the institutional capacity to implement exchange controls, it may be possible to arrest capital flight without an interruption in debt service and other contractual obligations. But this will depend on the severity of the crisis and the institutional capacity of the member. In circumstances where it is necessary to interrupt external debt service, it would be important for the authorities to put in place a framework for the eventual normalization of creditor relations by nonsovereign debtors, in order to minimize the long-term impact on corporations' market access. Such a framework could include two key features. First, the facilitation of an out-of-court workout mechanism operating in the shadow of domestic bankruptcy. Second, a specification of the minimum terms under which foreign exchange would be made available to service restructured debts.

The question arises, however, as to whether an SDRM should be designed to provide limited legal protection (in the form of a stay) during the period of renegotiation to domestic enterprises that might otherwise be subject to litigation as a result of the default arising from the imposition of controls.

It should be noted at the outset that, even if the decision were made to exclude nonsovereign debt from the coverage of an SDRM, exchange controls would still provide considerable legal protection in at least two respects. First, any restrictions imposed on the ability of residents or nonresidents to make transfers abroad would still be enforceable within the territory of the sovereign. Second, in the event that the controls give rise to payments arrears, foreign creditors would be precluded from enforcing their claims against a resident debtor in the territory of the sovereign. The legal protection that may *not* be provided by the controls would be protection against the enforcement of claims by nonresidents with respect to a resident debtor's assets that are located overseas. It is this latter category of protection that an SDRM could be designed to provide.[6]

[6]As interpreted by the courts of some IMF members, Article VIII, Section 2(b) of the IMF's Articles may be invoked to stay creditor enforcement against debtors unable to service their external payments because of exchange controls that are consistent with the IMF's Articles.

Among the complex issues that would arise if an SDRM were to apply to exchange controls is the feasibility of making a distinction between those debtors that, except for exchange controls, would be able to service their debt, and other debtors that are not healthy and need to be restructured. While it would be reasonable for the former category to enjoy some temporary legal protection under an SDRM, it would be preferable to make the latter category subject to the local insolvency law. A second difficulty relates to the protection of creditor interests. During the period of the stay on litigation, what measures could be put in place that would give creditors the assurance that the debtor is not using the stay as a means of facilitating asset stripping?

A final question relates to the role of the IMF. As discussed above, in the context of sovereign indebtedness, it is possible to design a framework where the key decisions are made by the majority of creditors rather than the IMF. However, in the context of exchange controls that gives rise to the default of a multitude of debtors (each with their own group of creditors), such an approach would not be feasible. In these circumstances, the legal authority to approve a temporary stay, if that were deemed an eventual feature of a new statutory mechanism, would need to reside with the IMF.

Conclusion

The absence of a robust legal framework for sovereign debt restructuring generates important costs. Sovereigns with unsustainable debts often wait too long before they seek a restructuring, leaving both their citizens and their creditors worse off. And when sovereigns finally do opt for restructuring, the process is more protracted than it needs to be and less predictable than creditors would like.

The international financial system lacks an established framework for restructuring that is equitable across all of the sovereign's creditors. There are few effective tools to address potential collective action problems that threaten to undermine restructuring agreements acceptable to the debtor and most of its creditors. Holdout creditors may be able to use the threat of litigation to seek to avoid concessions that the majority have agreed to make.

All this explains why it is important for the official community, sovereign debtors, and market participants to discuss how to improve the sovereign debt restructuring process.

This paper has laid out a possible approach. An international legal framework could be created to allow a qualified majority of the sovereign's creditors to approve a restructuring agreement, and to make that decision of the majority binding on a minority. The vote would need to include all the relevant creditors of the sovereign, not just the holders of a single debt instrument. Broadening the majority voting process beyond a single debt instrument vastly simplifies the process of creditor coordination, and would facilitate the negotiation of a deal that treats all creditors fairly. This approach draws on the principles of well-designed corporate bankruptcy regimes, and is similar in concept to the decision-making procedures among holders of a single bond issue that contains a majority restructuring clause.

Provisions for majority action would be most effective if supported by three other features, all of which protect the debtor's assets and capacity to pay while it works with its creditors to reach an agreement. The features are: a stay on creditor litigation after the suspension of payments; mechanisms that protect creditor interests during the stay; and the provision of seniority for fresh financing by private creditors. A single body would need to oversee the process of verifying claims and to resolve any disputes.

In such a framework, the decision whether to give legal protection for the sovereign and provide seniority for new private financing could to be left to the debtor and a qualified majority of its creditors. Similarly, the sovereign and a qualified majority of creditors would agree on the the terms of the ultimate restructuring. The primary purpose of an amendment of the IMF's Articles would be to provide the statutory legal basis to make an agreement between the debtor and the requisite majority of creditors binding on all relevant creditors.

There are a number of questions that would need to be fleshed out before such an approach could be made operational. Perhaps most crucial, and also most difficult, is the scope of the debt to be included in the voting process. It will also be important to explore with debtors and market participants how best to protect general creditor interests during the negotiating process, as well as how to structure the dispute resolution process.

These questions will not be easy to answer. But it is important not to shy away from the challenge. There is now widespread agreement that a new approach is necessary, and that a fairer, more efficient process for sovereign debt restructurings would represent a substantial strengthening of the international financial system. We should press ahead to achieve it.